Dedicated to all the librarians who have made the 1,000 Books Before Kindergarten challenge a success.

Congratulations, parents!

Your gift of reading will brighten your child's world!
It's never too early to open the reading door.

Your child will thank you!

Siouxland Libraries

# 1000 BOOKS
## Before Kindergarten

### A Promise and A Pledge

By Mark Borghese
& Charlie H. Luh

Illustrated by
Izzy Bean

I will read you 1,000 books
and maybe even more,

with colors and shapes
and daring escapes–
an ocean of books to explore.

I will read you 1,000 books
about belly buttons and knees,

with penguins and puppies
and baby fish guppies,
and three little mice that can't see.

I will read you 1,000 books
about children and babies
and mothers,

about picnics with ants,
that hide out in plants,
and families that love one another.

I will read you 1,000 books
about toucans, turtles, and tigers,

with stories of fun
and smiles and sun,
and great waterfalls and geysers.

I will read you 1,000 books
about a hungry bug
and a bad luck bunny,

with little red trucks,
that sometimes get stuck,
and bees and flowers and honey.

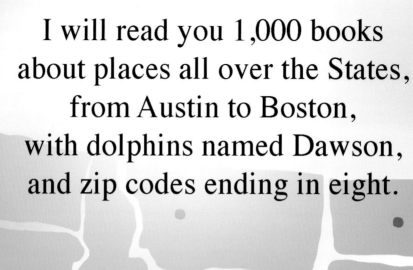

I will read you 1,000 books
about places all over the States,
from Austin to Boston,
with dolphins named Dawson,
and zip codes ending in eight.

I will read you 1,000 books
set in jungles and deserts and seas,
with singing giraffes
and songs about laughs,
and pirates with patches who sneeze.

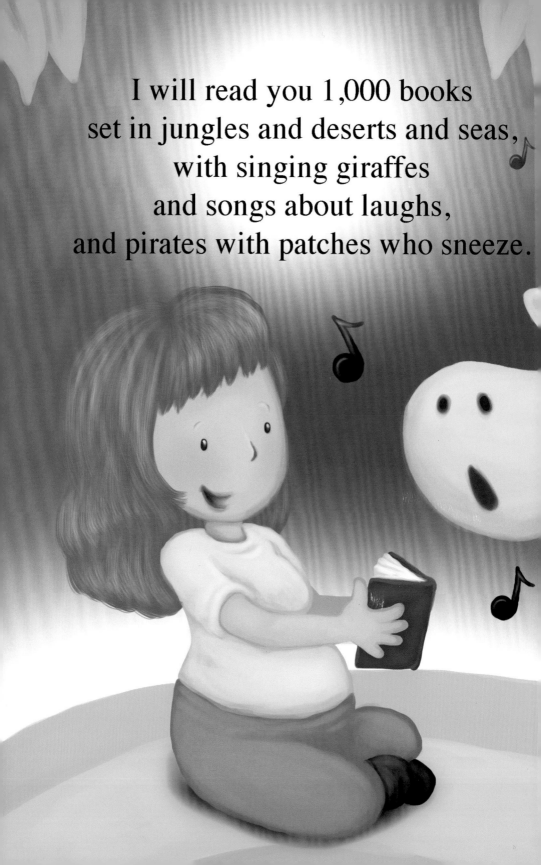

I will read you 1,000 books—
we'll travel to lands near and far,

from the capital of Peru to Timbuktu
by horseback, on trains, and in cars.

I will read you 1,000 books
about witches, goblins, and gnomes,

about green-eyed fairies
with magical berries,
and children just trying to get home.

I will read you 1,000 books
with talking cars and far away stars,

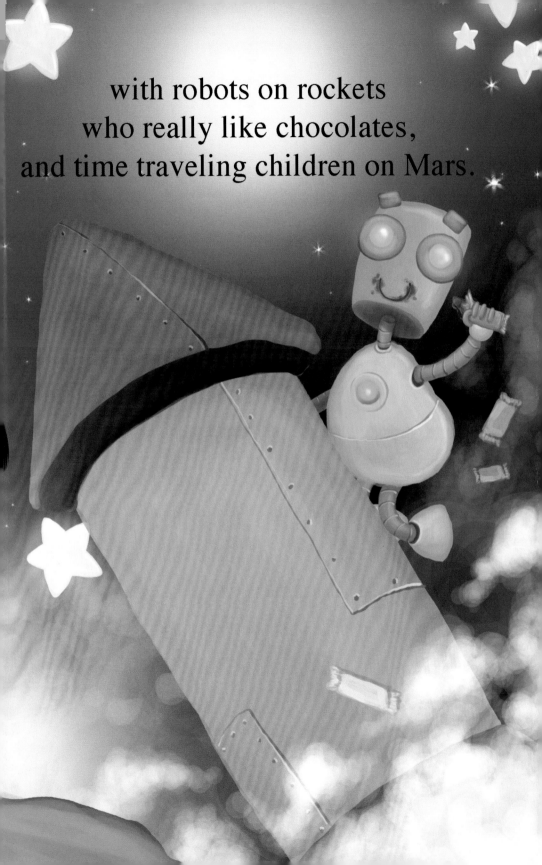

with robots on rockets
who really like chocolates,
and time traveling children on Mars.

I will read you 1,000 books
with addition, subtraction,
and rounding;
about the first day of school,
all the crazy and cool,
and growing up so fast,
it's astounding!

...la's ...

Griffin's book

Cruz's book

Aiden's book

Bennett's book

Parker's book

Joseph's book

Jordan's book

Niko's book

Kendall's book

Liam's book

Kelly's book

Diane's book

I will read you 1,000 books—
a promise, a pledge, a decree.

We will read every day,
and track all the way,
and soon you'll be reading to me!

Izzy Bean (www.izzybean.co.uk)

Since graduating from the University of Bolton in Greater Manchester, UK with a 1st class degree in illustration and animation, Izzy Bean has refined her drawing skills to provide professional illustrations in a fun and unique style. Izzy lives in Doncaster, UK and when she isn't drawing, she is reading or writing.

Mark Borghese (www.lvtv.com)

Mark received his Bachelor of Science in Commerce from the University of Virginia and his law degree from the University of Iowa College of Law. Mark lives in Las Vegas, Nevada with his genius wife and two children all of whom share a passion for learning, adventure, and lazy Sundays.

Charlie H. Luh (www.charlieluh.com)

Charlie received his undergraduate degree in Economics from The Johns Hopkins University and his law degree from the University of Iowa College of Law. Charlie currently resides in Nevada with his supportive wife and two energetic boys (one who has already completed the 1,000 Books Before Kindergarten challenge).